W9-DAX-739

WITHDRAWN

The Study of Money

Our Economy in Action

Tim Clifford

Rourke
Publishing LLC
Vero Beach, Florida 32964

www.rourkepublishing.com

PHOTO CREDITS: © Ford Media: page 4, 25 top; © Thorsten Rust, R. Gino Sana Maria; Sebastian Tomus, TheBand: page 5; © Radu Razvan: page 6; © Lisa F. Young: page 7; © Jim Lopes: page 8; © National Baseball Hall of Fame and Museum: page 9; © Library of Congress: page 10 top, 13; © Sue Smith: page 10 bottom; © Thomas M. Perkins: page 12; © Ken Mellott: page 14; © Rick Blythe: page 15; © Bianda Ahmad Hisham: page 16; © Andre Blais: page 18; © Glen Jones: page 19 bottom; © US Air Force - Tech. Sgt. Ben Bloker: page 20 top; © Keith Muratori: page 20 bottom; © Scott Rothstein: page 21; Scott S./ Glass Window: page 23; © Mark Winfrey, © Rafael Ramirez Lee, © Anyka: page 25; © Jonathan Larsen: page 26; © US Federal Reserves: page 27; © Emin Kuliyev: page 30 top, © Rafael Ramirez Lee: page 30 bottom

Editor: Jeanne Sturm

Cover Design: Renee Brady

Page Design: Tara Raymo

Library of Congress Cataloging-in-Publication Data

Clifford, Tim, 1959-
  Our economy in action / Tim Clifford.
    p. cm. -- (The study of money)
  Includes index.
  ISBN 978-1-60472-405-9
  1. United States--Economic conditions--Juvenile literature. I. Title.
  HC103.C54 2009
  330.973--dc22
                                    2008011332

Printed in the USA

IG/IG

Table of Contents

What is the Economy?

Think of the many ways we use money. Companies use it to buy materials to make things. Banks lend it. People use it to buy their homes, food, and clothing. All of these things, and more, make up the United States economy.

4 The **economy** is the way a country handles its money.

Everyone participates in the economy. Every time you buy something from a store, or spend money on a movie ticket, you are part of the economy.

The United States economy is by far the largest in the world. It is more than twice as large as Japan's economy, which is the second largest. That means that we buy and sell more than any other country in the world.

The World's Largest Economies

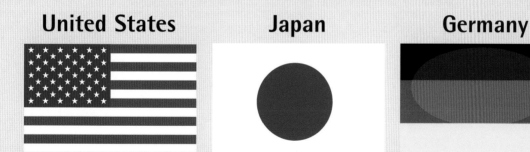

United States
13.2 Trillion Dollars

Japan
4.4 Trillion Dollars

Germany
2.9 Trillion Dollars

China
2.6 Trillion Dollars

United Kingdom
2.3 Trillion Dollars

5

All figures from the World Bank, 2006.

Goods and Services

There are two basic things bought and sold in this country: goods and services.

Goods are items that are sold. There are many types of goods. For example, household goods are items for the home, such as furniture and appliances. You will find canned goods and other items in the supermarket.

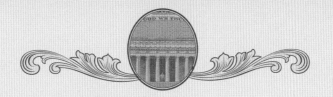

Services are also a large part of our economy. A **service** is work that helps others.

People who work in customer service don't produce any goods. Their job is to assist customers. Police, teachers, waiters, and many other professions all provide services.

Buying and Selling

In any economy, including ours, there are buyers and sellers.

The buyers are called **consumers**. Just about everyone is a consumer. If you buy or use anything at all, you are a consumer.

People who sell goods are called producers. They manufacture the things that consumers buy.

Supply and Demand

Have you ever wondered why a rare baseball card can be worth thousands of dollars, but a new pack of cards is quite inexpensive? The answer is supply and demand.

Supply is how much of something is available. Demand is the number of people who want it. These two things together help determine the price of any item.

If the supply is greater than the demand, the price goes down. If the demand is greater than the supply, the price goes up.

This rare Honus Wagner baseball card can sell for hundreds of thousands of dollars.

More Supply / Less Demand = Lower Price

Less Supply / More Demand = Higher Price

9

Trade

Many years ago, the main form of trade was a direct exchange. If you grew corn and needed wheat, you would exchange your

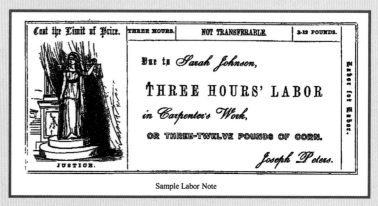

Sample Labor Note

corn directly with someone who grew wheat. Some forms of this type of trade still exist today.

Trade is the business of buying and selling goods. Most modern trade involves exchanging money for goods and services.

Shipping is the primary form of transportation for imported and exported goods.

10

No country can produce everything it needs. Countries trade with each other to get the goods and services they don't produce enough of.

To **import** goods is to bring them into a country. To **export** goods means to sell them to another country.

The United States imports far more goods than it exports. Even so, the U.S. is one of the leading exporters of goods in the world.

The five largest trading partners of the United States are Canada, China, Mexico, Japan, and Germany.

11

Employment

In a strong economy, most people are able to find jobs. When people have jobs, they can spend money. When they spend money, the economy grows. If not enough people can find employment, or work, the economy can slow down.

The unemployment rate shows the percentage of workers who are without a job. A rate of about 5 percent is considered normal.

If an economy stops growing for a short period of time, we call it a recession. When it stops growing for a long time, we call it a depression.

Find Out About...

The Great Depression

On October 29, 1929, the stock market crashed. This event began what is known as *The Great Depression*. Overnight, companies went out of business and millionaires lost their fortunes. Many people lost their jobs. The United States economy collapsed. It took more than a decade for the depression to end.

One of the worst effects of The Great Depression was on jobs. Before the depression, the unemployment rate was less than 4 percent. By 1933, almost one quarter, or 25 percent, of American workers were unemployed.

The Stock Market

Did you know that you can own a part of some of the biggest companies in the world? The **stock market** is the place where you can buy **shares**, or parts, of companies.

When a company makes a lot of money, the stock price goes up. **Investors**, the people who buy shares in the company, also make money. They can sell their shares for more than they paid for them.

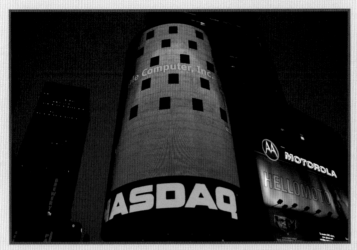

A stock exchange is where people buy and sell stocks. The two major exchanges in the United States are the NYSE and the NASDAQ.

The NYSE is the New York Stock Exchange. This is the largest stock exchange in the world. The companies that trade on the NYSE are worth more money combined than any other exchange. Stocks are bought and sold on the trading floor. There is a great deal of commotion as buyers and sellers trade stocks in person.

The NASDAQ stands for the National Association of Securities Dealers Automated Quotations. The NASDAQ was the world's first fully electronic stock exchange. More than 3000 companies now trade their stocks there.

Of course, stock prices don't always go up. If a company does poorly, its stock price will go down. Investors can lose some or all of their money.

The stock market used to be mostly for wealthy people. Today, many more people own stocks. Computers have made trading stocks easy for everyone. You can buy and sell stocks online.

If you are ever in New York City, you may want to pay a visit to Wall Street. Located in lower Manhattan, it is the center of economic activity in the United States.

Wall Street is the home of a number of famous stock exchanges, including the NYSE and the NASDAQ. Many major companies also have Wall Street addresses.

The New York Stock Exchange is located in a beautiful marble building at Wall and Broad Streets.

Real Estate

Another important part of the United States economy is **real estate**. This includes land and all the buildings on that land.

For many Americans, real estate is their biggest investment. They put a lot of money into buying their own houses.

The American Dream

The idea that if you work hard you can succeed is called the *American Dream*. Most people consider owning a home to be a big part of that dream. Today, more than 75 million Americans are homeowners. For many, the American Dream has become a reality.

Building new homes helps the economy a great deal. Each new home built puts a lot of people to work. Architects, electricians, plumbers, construction workers, and others are needed. A lot of money also gets spent on materials for the new home.

Taxes

The United States government provides many services to its citizens. Some of the things the government helps pay for are the military, highways, and healthcare services.

State and city governments provide local services. Police, firefighters, teachers, and parks department workers are mostly paid by local government.

To pay for services, governments use taxes. A **tax** is money that people and businesses must pay in order to support a government.

Everyone pays taxes in one way or another. Whenever goods and services are bought, sold, or traded, they are subject to being taxed.

Types of Taxes

There are many types of taxes. Some of the largest are:

Income tax: This is a tax charged on money you earn. The government keeps a percentage of a person's earnings.

Sales tax: When you buy something, you may be charged a sales tax. This is a percentage of the price of the item you buy.

Property tax: This is a tax on the value of your home.

Other taxes: We also pay taxes when we pay tolls, inheritance taxes, and gift taxes.

Benjamin Franklin

Benjamin Franklin once said, "In this world nothing can be said to be certain, except death and taxes." He meant that taxes have existed for centuries, and will probably always exist. While few people like paying taxes, everyone is required to pay them by law.

Taxes can help the economy. They help pay for things that people need, and they put people to work. Still, there is a lot of debate about how much the government should tax people. Higher taxes mean more government services, but lower taxes leave more money for people to spend.

The IRS

The IRS stands for the Internal Revenue Service. This branch of the United States Treasury Department was formed in 1862 to help collect taxes to pay for the Civil War. In 1895, the Supreme Court ruled that income taxes were unconstitutional.

In 1913, the income tax was restored by the 16th Amendment to the Constitution. Since that time, the IRS has been in charge of collecting income tax. It also investigates individuals and businesses who fail to pay. The IRS Headquarters is in Washington, D.C.

Inflation

Can you imagine a time when a loaf of bread cost ten cents, or a new car cost under $500? Both of those were real prices of goods in the United States many decades ago. What happened? Why do things cost so much more today?

The answer is inflation. **Inflation** is a general increase in prices. This usually doesn't hurt the economy, because people earn more over time, as well. Sometimes, however, inflation can rise too fast. Items begin to cost more than people can afford to pay. When this happens, people try to spend less. This slows the economy.

Because of inflation, many items cost a lot more today than they did years ago. Here are some examples:

Item	Cost Then	Cost Now
A New Car	In 1915, the Model T Ford cost about $450.	Today, a new car can cost $15,000 and higher.
A New Home	In 1975, the average cost of a new home was less than $45,000.	Today, the average price is greater than $300,000.
A Movie Ticket	In 1985, a movie ticket cost about $3.00.	Today, a ticket can cost $12.00 or more.
A Bottle of Soda	In 1940, a 12-ounce bottle of soda cost about 5 cents.	Today, a bottle of soda can cost more than $1.50.

25

Federal Reserve

Also called *the Fed*, the Federal Reserve is the central bank of the United States. One of the main jobs of the Federal Reserve is to keep inflation in check. Another important role is to try to keep interest rates low.

Low interest rates cause people and companies to borrow more. They then spend this borrowed money. This can help the economy to grow. If interest rates are too low, inflation can rise and hurt the economy.

It is the job of the Fed to balance interest rates and inflation.

26

There are twelve branches of the Federal Reserve spread across America. The leaders of these branches make up the Board of Governors. One is selected by the president to serve as Chairman.

Meet an Important Person...

Alan Greenspan

Alan Greenspan was appointed Fed Chairman in 1987 and served for twenty years, longer than any other chairman in history. Shortly after he was appointed, one of the largest stock market crashes in United States history occurred. On Monday, October 19, 1987, also known as Black Monday, the U.S. stock market fell over 20 percent. Greenspan and the Fed helped the economy survive that event.

Greenspan was still chairman during the dot-com era of the 1990s. The words dot-com refer to how Internet companies are named. In the mid to late 1990s, these companies, along with other stocks, increased greatly in price. Greenspan warned that these prices were a bubble waiting to burst. By the year 2000, they did. Many of those Internet companies went out of business.

27

Measuring the Economy

It is important to know whether the economy is growing or shrinking. A growing economy is healthy. A shrinking economy is usually a sign of trouble.

One way to measure the economy is by GDP. This stands for Gross Domestic Product. It equals the total amount of goods and services produced in a year.

GDP= Total Value of Goods + Total Value of Services

The United States measures GDP quarterly, or four times a year. An increase of around 3 percent a year is considered healthy growth.

Federal Government Fiscal Year	
First quarter	*October - December*
Second quarter	*January - March*
Third quarter	*April - June*
Fourth quarter	*July - September*

Some other ways to measure the economy include:

Report Name	What it Measures
Consumer Price Index (CPI)	This measures the price of ordinary items a household might use.
Producer Price Index (PPI)	This measures the price of materials companies use to make products.
Existing Home Sales	This is a measure of the sales of homes that have already been lived in. This is useful because people buy homes when the economy is healthy.
Retail Sales	This is a measure of the dollar value of products sold to people. It shows whether people are buying things, which is a sign of a healthy economy.

The Global Economy

Years ago, most U.S. companies sold goods and services primarily to Americans. Because of technology, it is now much easier to buy and sell goods and services around the world. This gives our economy new ways to grow. It may also mean our own economy depends more and more on how the world economy performs.

Our economy is always in action. With the global economy, we can expect the economy to change in new and exciting ways.

Glossary

consumers (kuhn-SOO-murz): people who buy and use products and services

economy (i-KON-uh-mee): the way a country handles its money

export (EK-sport): to send goods to another country to be sold there

goods (GUDZ): items that are sold

import (IM-port): to bring goods into a country

inflation (in-FLAY-shuhn): a general increase in prices

investors (in-VEST-ors): people who give or lend money to a company with the belief that they will get more money back in the future

real estate (REEL ess-TATE): land and the buildings that are on it

service (SUR-viss): work that helps others

shares (SHAIRZ): many equal parts into which the ownership of a business is divided

stock market (STOK MAR-kit): a place where stocks and shares in companies are bought and sold

tax (TAKS): money that people and businesses must pay in order to support a government

trade (TRADE): the business of buying and selling goods.

31

Index

Further Reading

Davidson, Avelyn. *The Bull and the Bear: How Stock Markets Work.* Children's Press, 2007.

Gilman, Laura Ann. *Economics (How Economics Works).* Lerner Publications, 2005.

Loewen, Nancy. *Taxes, Taxes!: Where the Money Goes.* Picture Window Books, 2005.

Websites

www.federalreserve.gov/kids/default.htm

www.irs.gov/app/understandingTaxes/servlet/IWT1L1ol

www.library.thinkquest.org/3096/

About the Author

Tim Clifford is an educational writer and the author of many nonfiction children's books. He has two wonderful daughters and two energetic Border Collies that he adopted from a shelter. Tim became a vegetarian because of his love for animals. He is also a computer nut and a sports fanatic. He lives and works in New York City as a public school teacher.